Fragments of a Nocturne

Fragments of a Nocturne

Mark Blaeuer

White Violet Press

© 2014 Mark Blaeuer. All rights reserved. This material may not be reproduced in any form, published, reprinted, recorded, performed, broadcast, rewritten or redistributed without explicit permission of Mark Blaeuer. All such actions are strictly prohibited by law.

ISBN: 978-0692277201

Cover Art: h.koppdelaney @ Photo Flickr

Kelsay Books
White Violet Press
www.kelsaybooks.com

for Sharon

Acknowledgments

My sincere gratitude goes out to numerous literary journal editors, who first published this work (some of the poems originally appeared in a slightly different form).

Angle: "Deeply Felt," "Parable," "Patience," "Winter Journal: Stray Facts"
Antiphon: "Meanwhile, Back at the Ranch"
Astropoetica: "The Reverend's Fantasy"
Avocet: "The Gods"
The Barefoot Muse: "Lessons in Period"
BUZZwords: "Easter," "Improvements"
The Camel Saloon: "Jeremiad," "Oppressive, 1973," "Proof," "Sundial"
The Centrifugal Eye: "Fable"
Chrysanthemum: "Incursion"
Crowdancing: "Artist," "Hotel Ruins"
The Dark Horse: "Bucolic," "From the Analects"
The Edge City Review: "Cedar Grove, 1982"
Fauquier Poetry Journal: "Water"
The Flea: "Discovery of a Literary Artifact," "Methought I Saw My Late A-Soused Haint," "The Peasant Skims His Glossy Catalogue,"
Gryphon: "Big Stump Basin, 1981"
The Hiram Poetry Review: "Remains"
Hobble Creek Review: "Old Quarry"
IthacaLit: "Fragments of a Nocturne"
Lucid Rhythms: "Blessing of the Stones," "Legendary"
Lucidity: "Birthright," "Visiting an Old Friend"
The Lyric: "Allies at the Feeder"
The Montucky Review: "Tableau"
Nimrod: "The Grand Exhibition"
Paintbrush: "Leafing through the Bible on a Winter's Morning"

Parnassus Literary Journal: "On Trap Mountain after Work, 1997"
Piedmont Literary Review: "To a Friend in Wilderness"
Pivot: "A Colloquy of Sorts," "The Voice in No Man's Land"
Potpourri: "Lure"
The Raintown Review: "Modern Ranger"
RE:AL: "Lunch at the Growing Addition"
The Road Not Taken: "Single Pen"
The Rotary Dial: "Another on the Loose"
Shit Creek Review: "Eclogue, with Sofa"
Shot Glass Journal: "Shrapnel"
Slant: "The Keeper"
The Small Pond: "Clay"
TAPJoE: "Hillside"
Tilt-a-Whirl: "Advice to a Profiteer," "Ballade of the Danged"
Verse Wisconsin: "Undines and Rednecks"
Westview: "Moving Still Life"
Wind: "The Road Taken"

Six of these poems were reprinted in the following literary journals, whose editors I also thank:

Pirene's Fountain: "Easter"
Pudding: "Artist"
Umbrella: "Modern Ranger," "The Road Taken"
The Victorian Violet Press & Journal: "Lure," "To a Friend in Wilderness"

Contents

Acknowledgments

Remains	13
Discovery of a Literary Artifact	14
Patience	15
Cedar Grove, 1982	17
Clay	18
Another on the Loose	19
Blessing of the Stones	20
Visiting an Old Friend	21
The Peasant Skims His Glossy Catalogue	22
Allies at the Feeder	23
Leafing through the Bible on a Winter's Morning	24
Winter Journal: Stray Facts	25
Easter	26
The Reverend's Fantasy	27
From the Analects	28
Bucolic	29
Undines and Rednecks	30
Tableau	31
Eclogue, with Sofa	32
Lunch at the Growing Addition	33
Hotel Ruins	34
Single Pen	35
Incursion	36
Improvements	37
On Trap Mountain after Work, 1997	39
The Gods	40
Hillside	41
Moving Still Life	42
Old Quarry	43
To a Friend in Wilderness	44

Meanwhile, Back at the Ranch	45
Fragments of a Nocturne	46
Deeply Felt	47
The Keeper	48
Oppressive, 1973	49
Artist	50
Water	51
Ballade of the Danged	52
Lessons in Period	53
Legendary	54
Modern Ranger	55
Big Stump Basin, 1981	56
A Colloquy of Sorts	57
Advice to a Profiteer	59
The Grand Exhibition	60
The Voice in No Man's Land	61
Sundial	63
Shrapnel	64
Birthright	65
Parable	66
Fable	67
Jeremiad	68
Proof	69
The Road Taken	70
Lure	71
Methought I Saw My Late A-Soused Haint	72

About the Author

Remains

Examining a field notebook,
I noticed photographs of Betty Fry
(she appeared 21 or 22,
a cigarette in hand).
One especially
striking picture had this caption:
"Why the 1931 University of Chicago
Survey of Fulton County
was successful." In it,
she was looking at a copper
projectile with flanged tang, in situ.
She wore a dark scarf,
evidently blue.
I recognized instructors—
despite plus fours, austere.
Lengthening effect
were other photos snapped of visitors,
the women in vanilla fashions,
men in dapper suits.
Not surprising
were collegiate grins on tan bucks
later to be patriarchs themselves,
now dead or tolerated
by technicians
(labeled,
inventoried).

Discovery of a Literary Artifact

Like nothing else in Tennessee,
that jar sat for awhile.
The lid was off, though, and a bee
attracted by the physic smile

of sun on glass fell in
and drowned in the rainwater there.
Next, mold and algae, then
a buttercup. This colony of air

and nutrients and light
held out for decades. Jimmy Ray
located it last week, and he knew right
fast where to go: eBay,

the mystery—so coy—
already on a shelf in Illinois.

Patience

A 1957 radio,
half-buried in the humus and new-fallen
leaves and seedpods (muddy, rootleted
dial hopeful in its dual Conelrad
mindset, bulb-lit triangle-in-a-circle,
640 and 1240 kilohertz),
has met the common telos after all.
These tubes are shot, though, wires rusted through
where field mice gnawed the insulation off.
A pleasure to endow the ages with
it must have been, and now the resurrection
turns on yet another seeming end:
an archeologist's retirement,
a walk on his own twice-owned property.
There is no need to excavate, but habit
serves a man or woman equally
if death intrude.
             His trowel, just put away
and older than some objects wheedled under
its point, scrapes in a lovely rhythm here
at this congeries of domestic waste.
The man hauls every patient artifact
back to the house he lives in, where she lived
before he met her, cleans and reconstructs
a hybrid dinosaur, available
transistors well-ignored, the company
extinct as symbolized with model name:
a Casket. So, in propagating care
that obviates a skill, and buying off
an online source components earth had not
preserved, he manages to fix his thought
on distant record hops.

                    The radio
adorns a wooden shelf she used to dust.
The queen is mute. A daughter will inherit
monsters, always, even if they sing
to outdo Robeson. Good auctioneers
depend on this.

Cedar Grove, 1982

*A crew of twelve from the Arkansas Archeological
Survey relocated 79 graves from a historic Black cemetery
threatened by revetment construction. Analysis dated all
graves to the period 1890 to1927 when the cemetery was
covered by silt from a major flood. High frequencies of
degenerative joint disease on the adult skeletons suggest a
hard rigorous life style.*—J.C. Rose, ed., *Gone To A Better Land*

Swollen with dead cows, televisions, whole
trees, the Red River slurried behind us.
One entropic principle—*doom*—stole
shoreline to Gulf of Mexico. That, plus
cottonmouths in black tarpaulined pits
after breakfast, cast the eidetic spell.

Our aims entirely straightforward, our transits
plumb, we meant science. That ephemeral
June (three weeks to spade, trowel, brush, analyze,
load in huge coffins our 79
pitiful bone piles) twelve pairs of eyes
ached, overseers to a hard design.

Land, time . . . gone over Jordan years ago,
my form a slender rampart against flow.

Clay

A brick 8½ by 4 by 2
sits on the wicker table next to me.
On the brick: two curved lines connected to
a pair of shorter straight incisions meant—
and instantly perceived—to be a bird.
This crude, baked thing was found amid remains
of my wife's great grandfather's cotton farm
near Princeton, Arkansas. There Pappy owned
slaves; one of them undoubtedly made this.

There was a real bird also, and it flew.

Another on the Loose

Born white in L.A., in an obstetric ward,
he's proud to wear a Plains-style headdress, chant,
and gather more disciples to his tribe
like eagle feathers trafficked on the sly

or even budgie feathers. Either way,
he says his people are real Indians
with sobriquets he formalized: Sharp Hair,
Nice Butterfly, and Iridescent Girl.

He argues they were loud for generations
prior to Cassidy, LaRue, or Mix.
Ancestors, he explains, would yell a warning
in an aspen-wooded amphitheater,

then spark a flint to burn the underbrush.
Nowadays, he chuckles, there's no need
to strike a match or flick some butane lighter.
According to this sage, all ancient flame

evolved to Spirit. Turns out he's Sedona-
certified to sense, placate, and use
incendiary life. Therefore, the crowd
is safe when he shouts "Fire!" from one aisle

of the multiplex at Sylvan Acres Mall,
and it's wrong to persecute his gentle faith,
especially with everybody hot
to catch a midnight showing of *Billy Jack*.

Blessing of the Stones

He took his gem collection to a priest
for "Blessing of the Stones," a new event
the church had real hope for. And sure enough,
a hundred people stood in line with jade
and garnet, rosy quartz and travertine.
He thought, "Because the stones are not concerned
about survival, beauty lives." He thought,
"I carry, in my body, minerals
a chicken or a cauliflower used."
The queue had dwindled. Stammering hello,
he felt a spray of consecrated water,
one part oxygen, two hydrogen,
react with his own sudden tears. The priest,
astounded, felt: for the first time in years.

Visiting an Old Friend

He shows, proudly, his own handiwork:
a wooden thingamajig, deftly used,
ekes out the Gallinaceous Lexicon
to coax wild turkey into hunter's range.
He marketed and became slave to this
device, unable to meet huge demand.
Now he's let retailers go, can spend
a summer day on something easier
than oak. I ask about his wife, "How's Ruth?"
"Ruth who?" Hadn't heard of his divorce,
been away too long. But pain is relative.
Seven years ago, in his front yard
with goggles, gloves, earplugs, electric shears,
he assaulted overgrown hedge until
an itch in one leg made him stop: the air
full, his body stung by yellow jackets.
He scoffs, "I'd rather deal with that ten times
than have to pass another kidney stone."

The Peasant Skims His Glossy Catalogue

On a raw March day—I wouldn't mind
if spring this year were a tad premature—
I run across an ad for a boxed set
of eighteen DVDs showing the czars'
art collection at the Hermitage.

I never splurge, ordinarily,
but now the wind cuffs our bungalow,
and flurries of diaphanous insects—
of tiny span—descend from mating flight
to ragged lawn, melt under, a deep loss . . .

It's over. Though I can't quite be accused
of furthering a wish for Romanov
execution, nonetheless I serve
as witness. Here is the official knell,
plus my Visa expiration date.

Allies at the Feeder

The titmouse and the chickadee
take turns, each flying in to rest
a second—one seed—harmony
between two species manifest.

If only we two on this side
of window glass were equally
in concert. I watch, edified,
our tabby cat's own reverie:

to me it's hope and feathered words,
to Emmy a buffet of birds.

Leafing through the Bible on a Winter's Morning

Above a line of seemingly dead branches,
the sap as quiet and as powerful
as hieroglyphics (thank Champollion)
no preacher dares to read, the sun emerges

as a self-sufficient dynamo.
There is no deity required here,
no id, I AM, or hybrid Phaeton:
no sons. Icicles glow, reflecting red,

as if they were an insect's compound eye,
the image multiplied a thousandfold.
It's obvious, no Nordic would define
a reservoir of fire as a hell—

it brightens every solitary thing.
These pages don't; they're only good for kindling.

Winter Journal: Stray Facts

"I have now found the law of the oak leaves,"
wrote Hopkins on the 19th of July,
the year of his Lord 1866.
I, on the other hand, see only sticks
devoid of life. Pathetic alibi,
cerebral chemistry no pill relieves
in truth. Although our morning is "v. fine,"
the dog and I are weighted to a chair.
A dying larva in a chrysalis,
however, yields more energy than this
heft in a green recliner. Everywhere,
linoleum is lit with the divine
spark, so cliché, of a bacterium
to which my dog and I will yet succumb.

Easter

Warmth to all
life, life
inferring June,
the crimson meadow,
sailor navigating via
polestar hive.

Ancestors move.
Now a light
green
tone hallows,
bloodroot
in the soil's

choir stirring
melismatic
awe to coloratura,
faith
in the body
temporal.

The Reverend's Fantasy

If I were to imagine Yahweh's throne
directly overhead (or, likelier,
out at the apex of our thinly known
Orion Arm), it wouldn't halt the stir
of sky in hemoglobin oxygen.
A reddened lamp hurls photons in night air
a toggle switch redarkens, yang and yin—
we sense another realm beyond Altair.
Unhampered, thank God, by an easy moon,
and peering at a smudge M. Messier
called 31, my eyes adjust, and soon
the finder scope stops at a live display:
Andromeda chained, left on a rocky strand,
the spiral galaxy in her right hand.

From the Analects

I slump in a recliner, with Dufay
drawn through satellite on the ides
of December, wondering if I deployed
enough insulation at the pumphouse
for 2-inch PVC not to freeze,
in case tonight's as cold as the Weather
Channel predicted. Today good water
pressure let me shower the invisible
shards of fiberglass off my arms
(I had to wrestle, awkwardly, each nasty
roll). Since then, hours of anemic glaze.
Evening strides up like Confucius.
In a classic translation—Arthur Waley?
James Ware?—the Master enjoined his followers
to respect whoever they meet, yet,
he said, if a man has attained the age
of 50 and done little of real worth,
abuse him. An immortal sage is dashing in
with a stick and a shout as if to scatter crows:
"Hey, old fool, cut the stupor! I mean now!"
The blood slows.

Bucolic

In 1963 United Artists
released a 45 by Country Johnny
Mathis. Side A, a certified non-hit?
"Thinkin' Too Far Behind." That and the flip
he yowled affectedly in a high twang
embedded in the amber of vinylite.

Two people at their cabin years ago,
priming a leaking pump. Our wee hour chore:
cold fingers, balky valves, a dim flashlight.
Street-dumb, we failed as born-again hayseed.
I grieve, though, remembering an orchid
that brightened the sawdust path to our springhouse.

Undines and Rednecks

En la región oculta de las ninfas
El sesgo rayo a penetrar alcanza
Y alumbra al pie de despeñadas linfas
De las ondinas la nocturna danza.
　　—José Asunción Silva (1865-1896), "Las Ondinas"

Within the realm where nymphs enthrall,
a slanted ray illumines scenes
below a limpid waterfall:
the nightly dance of fair undines.

And three'll get you two, some guys
are readying a net to drop
smack dab on the ballet, their eyes
a visual barbaric yawp.

If Walt were there, I wager he'd
disguise himself as manna-grass
around the pool. As for the greed
of idiots, it may surpass

what elemental fumblers do
when beauty stares them in the face.
Or not. Lest any misconstrue
my nugget: screw the human race.

Tableau

In a flea market near
Spoon River, the proprietor
critiques E.L. Masters: "That gossip?
Look,

this is poetry." The old fellow kneels,
takes a mildewed
gilt-edge book
from under a wobbly table-leg.

Eclogue, with Sofa

The odour of the burning couch is carried across
the meadows from the lately-ploughed stubble . . .
　　　—Richard Jefferies, *Hodge and his Masters*

The furniture's in milo, smoldering.
Twelve years go by. Astride lunch counter stools,
he-men taunt the field's owner: "Is that thing
still burnin', Bobby Joe?" They grin like ghouls.

"I reckon so." An east coast curator,
in town for an azalea festival
with his wife, overhears and dares to utter:
"Let me buy it." Guffaws, inscrutable.

Then Bobby Joe speaks up: "I reckon you
did," causing a young hiree to drop
her plate of ham and navy beans. A few
eyes look at the wife, who says: "Bobby, stop."

Lunch at the Growing Addition

An hour to sprawl in duff and lichen, to
pluck a woodsy sourness in black-
berries almost pail-ripe. Sweet enough.
Blue-gray gnatcatchers dart through scrub hawthorn,
stunted oak. A vulture overhead.
Power saws whine. Trucks haul the jumbly fill
a Neo-Colonial needs to perch on steep
mountainside. Tourist-commuters ride
to and from the airport in our valley.
Grasshoppers fly in sunshine, a few yards,
foraging. *Liatris*, blazing star,
empurples a common hill. Brown and yellow
butterflies—no idea what species,
didn't bring a field guide—are manic,
barely in time to join the color. I
flick away thin (as yet) ticks caught descending
trousers, tickling skin. The brain likewise
crawls to appointments, a capillary flush
with the cholesterol of revenue.

Hotel Ruins

Angst, a foreigner usurps a niche. I continue
   up the path sandwiched between larkspur,
   phlox.

Onto a palisade, Denver below. Less smog (Sunday).
   Glorious, Muir'd fondly intone.

On plateau. Crunch rubble to a chimney, a trun-
   cated butte. Hearth buckled. Luxuriant
   undergrowth: a plastic bag; some Wrigley's
   wadded in one crevice.

North, freight rumbles across mountainside into
   a tunnel.

Single Pen

Varnished inside the cabin, these pine logs
chant in the umber dialect of sky
at sunset over Shiloh Mountain; of fog
enveloping Lost Peak, suffusing Dry
Fork hollow with air-water at sunrise.
Each adze mark is a genuine effect—
rough hewn, no modules for the builder's clan.
Spirits molder in their resinous eyes,
knots and pegs where branches have been hacked
away, blunt vestiges of rural men.

I'm unrelated, shadow on the tongue,
here to bow to a ready-made rainbow.
Who's lonely? Not some bluffer dangling
his feet in heaven, happy as Thoreau
atop Fair Haven Hill. An emerald
glow hints of earth. On weekends of escape
to quiet reparation, I hike down
to Thomas Creek with dogs who come when called,
obedient to joy. The proper shape
and heft of solitude are, at last, won.

First, realtors earn a commission. In
law, deeds convey land; human acts redeem
the ownership. I rake leaves, and gray stone
foundations iterate to me their dream
of eaves and shingles, walls and furniture.
I rest inside with coffee, marmalade
on toast. Then I'm out to split hickory
and oak for an investiture of fire
in blood and domicile. An ideal trade:
to pay too much, a pittance, and go free.

Incursion

Woodrat homesteading
engine, hickory nut shells
on the battery.

Improvements

This entrance walk
evolved ground to roof
to ground. Ocean bed uprose, wore
down to hills,
a jack of rustic trade who prized and mortared
stone,
a plume settling in valley.
Pine logs held the ashes' warmth
emitted at fireplace

destined to be sealed.
One day
men carried a potbelly stove
in, fit sheet metal pipe onto cast iron,
out to flue.
A damper choked off draft,
teased a wispy smoke into flameburst
(wood the father
split with axe; son chose sledge and steel
cone).

Asthmatics bought the cabin,
installed a furnace.
Chimney served
to brace unwieldy antenna.
Shingles dethroned every lichened shake,
yet the old tower stood,

dismantled at leisure. Retired,
a couple
laid ancient wave-rib anew
in charming curve to gingerbread front door.

A decade later,
arson dealt the coup de grâce to a probated cot,
leaving an amorphous gray
lump Beethoven's Pastoral melted to,
briers hiding rock.

On Trap Mountain after Work, 1997

I lean my staff against novaculite
outcrop, sit. Breather for a would-be god.
How classical the Ouachitas, how right
for scuppernong to twine around the flawed
bole of an unusually hoar oak.
Bare Mountain on an 1891
map (cedar bald? fire? did a rail line stoke
cut-and-run?), now it's green as Helicon
in these few minutes of a dying sun.
Clambering up beside me: the bank loan
on this land, fax, computer, telephone . . .
Tomorrow's pointed at me like a gun,
and all I have for self-defense is my
knife-sharp belief that even the gods die.

The Gods

Mesa to each compass point.
Basalt, volcanic tuff, rhyolite
bare except for a dotting of juniper.
Water glints below.

Eight feet around and seventy tall,
a tree drowned years ago on the Río Grande
stands yet,
holding its red shore.

Hillside

> Wet
> the dead leaves stick upon the hillside
> —Lew Welch

October in the Ozarks. It's been dry;
the leaves, except for sumac and blackgum,
went straight from sickening green to earth's dust.
Faint wind blows here. Again I understand

Lew Welch, cross-legged, all across his lap
the shotgun of his future suicide.
According to his letters he performed
zazen that way. He's gone, one more stray thought.

Moving Still Life

Atop beveled clarity
at my left, one ladybug clings.
The good grey pickup
bumps along.

Old Quarry

The west is blood. Beneath,
pried or blasted slabs never to be dressed.
The dynamite and crowbar history.

Stone clinks on stone.
I peer through bifocals. Fifty yards off—
a big cat, black, impending

night. The feral pet or melanistic lion
picks a route down scree
and disappears in shadow long as the trail home.

To a Friend in Wilderness

Love is a habitat
of mind
high wanderlust
can never find.

Endangered feelings thrive
within
a stable heart, away
from din.

Repeat your vow,
a whippoorwill
as constant as the dusk
is still.

Meanwhile, Back at the Ranch

Adrenalin supported by caffeine,
no doubt a benefice to rodeo
clowns, helps in each attempt I make to save
my day when it's been thrown off by some bull,
e.g. a printer gone recalcitrant,
our baby eleemosynary in
his diapers, or activating supper
out of motley snippets in the fridge.
I'm superhuman in my casual
banana-yellow polka-dotted tie
of attitude. When she gets home, I'll have
a kiss, a hug, a sweet lobotomy:
the wrangler's medication that I crave.

Fragments of a Nocturne

Moon looms over a stethoscopic ray.
The ancient midwife
slaps night to chirrup, bay, and bloody life.
A burglar's-eye-view: aisles
lined with artifice, whitewashed valves.
Exoskeleton crew. A May beetle
hits window for light, the shine of elytra
beckoning mates.

Five recline:
one bald, one wearing a wig, one
turbaned in scarf, one with fine locks of second
growth, one virgin to loss. Technology
fills half their arms against the oft-imagined.
A corner-mounted TV drips evening
drama. Food commercials
nauseate a patient. The shuffle to toilet, rolling an IV
($7000 bag the size of a tumor, a tumor the size
of the moon).

Deeply Felt

We shared a pleasant day among the dead,
our tombstone-hallowed anniversary.
Crisscrossing, as we walked, unspirited
rows—each with its own arbor vitae tree—
and peering down where sunken ovals led
the eye to hope a casket handle might
flash in the sun, we did just what we said
we'd never do: feel sorry for these white
church-haunted bones. *Hand me the shovel, dear,
I'm quite myself again with dusk around.*
A crescent moon surprised us both, and we
kissed, intimating luck as in that night
long, long ago, our first time on a mound
of happy soil with no patrolman near.

The Keeper

Before she left,
the blonde blinked: "I don't like bees very well."
Sighing, he turned to me.
I wanted service. He sold me four jars,
then walked me to the gate,
one arm covered with *Hymenoptera*.
"Take nectar, make honey—that's all they do,"
he offered.
But he was wrong—
they can sting.

Oppressive, 1973

Dead hour. No change in the mercury
hellometer. Sleep ransacked. A red skull,
an inbred apparition. That locale
ground them out ex nihilo. Animate
leaves crackling as if under human weight—
recidivistic prowler shifting to
his haunches for an upward-angle show
past wind chime, holly. She sprang off the bed,
dressed lightning, scoured the gray neighborhood
until she finally became insensate.
The presence—close as fear, conjoined with hate—
stayed. Drone of air conditioners: a lie.

Artist

She'd announced,
"The only culture in this place is an active yeast infection."

Now she was bailing out—
trudging thirty-five miles to the local university.

She packed food and camping gear, then
set out on Highway 62.

Appalled by carcasses
of animals run over by cars,

she'd cradle the body of each victim
to the nearest roadsign,

where she'd drape
a distinctive breed of message.

Two days later
(after the Missing Person report),

the police discovered her ten miles out,
sobbing on the gravel shoulder,

a dead possum around her neck.
And they arrested her.

Water

With a white-flecked beard of several days, like markings
on a shell, he stands on littered night's beach.
He'd rather not, but water is compelling—
deep/shallow, salt/fresh, high tide and low ebb . . .

He knows each would-have-been sea dog on shore
poring over surf (he's one, concocting
terms reflective of the qualities
the water shares with sacrificial blood
and amniotic fluid—all in Greek).

He ponders hypothetical offspring
and fears they'll never mount the canvas needed
to catch their father's passion blowing lifeward.

The sun inches up. Thoughts dissipate . . .

He scans the horizon with binoculars.

No, nothing recognizable out there.

It's said a woman sailed out on the shelf,
dropped anchor. With provisions for a lifetime,
she stayed there—and her language turned to liquid,
for the ocean's vastness overwhelmed her.

He loves that legend as he does the neutral
black (unending in complexity).
The woman he respects, if she existed,
as he does the water that disturbs him
when it rises much above his ankles,

as he does the terrifying water.

Ballade of the Danged

Before you quit your dream of the guitar,
you almost learned a chord. You don't recall
which. Hormones were abducting you to far
and fateful territory: basketball.
Your dad erected goal and netting—tall
at five feet skyward of your height-to-be.
Coach uttered "You were cut," in study hall.
The words you spoke were hardly poetry.

You finished high school, and your registrar
at college had advice: "Well, freshmen all
take Freshman Comp." That's English-in-a-jar
to kids whose innards ached for alcohol
the frat boys vomited near keggers. Paul
McCartney died that year, supposedly,
and you were a campus DJ yet that fall.
The shtick you chose was hard on poetry

played backwards on KWLR.
They fired you. "We walk before we crawl,"
somebody said, so you bought a used car
and drove, in debt resplendent, to a mall,
where stag-juiced idiots worked up the gall
to proposition teens. You were just three
on a ten-scale, out for a perfect doll.
Your pick-up lines were hardly poetry.

Prints earned you a jumpsuit and a block wall
(a *nolo contendere* was your plea).
Thursday a writer visits: you're in thrall.
The lines you pen are hard-won poetry.

Lessons in Period

Music History: he emphasized
the Middle Ages' pre-polyphony
more than half a semester. By its end
we'd limped—barely—into High Baroque.
He read verbatim out of a textbook
and made us memorize its clotted prose,
but alter ego was much glitzier.

Sponsor of the college marching band,
he led them up a candy-strewn thoroughfare
each autumn at homecoming, uniformed.
One year, after triangles and drums
had shaken alumni flesh and Doppler effect
depressed their sound, an ambulance's siren
aired the arch power of dissonance.

In a crimson V-neck at Ireland Field,
the student senate rep, possessed of bleak
news, wrestled with the delicate: "He was
rushed to hospital, and . . . and . . . let us have
a moment of silence." Charging out, our assistant
football coach grabbed away the microphone
and, after feedback, verbalized harsh fact:

"I don't think you people understood.
He died. *Professor died.*" So there we had it—
blunt speech, offensive and defensive lines,
opposed to flowing monody in Latin
nobody understood when he gently placed
the needle at recorded Kyrie
in our classroom, a cortège in his heart.

Legendary

Infinity's annunciation deals
a blow to what some imp referred to as
the "better hours of malignant jazz."
But that was on the Suffolk coast. Your skill
solidified with every liquid phrase
you took off from. You flew a brazen horn
to fame, you buggered the empyrean,
and finally you landed in this corn:
the Hall of Ignominious Ash and Dust,
dead to your fertilizing legacy.
As if you were that alto saxophone,
its keys your many eyes into the sound
of darkness, rust in England's quaint debris,
a fossil of an avant-garde ideal.

Modern Ranger

I staff our information desk, deflect
all questions of a thorny nature—wrecked,

a once-upon-a-heaven nearly sold.
Yet this defines a good day: mere refold-

ing of a map, the concentrated talk
directing folks to Hullabaloo Rock.

A bad day forces me to hunch behind
the PC with a bureaucratic mind,

processing action-plans and memos, buzz
a caffeine drone. My first desire was

to share the beauty of a flower made
for love; to wander straight-backed, unafraid.

My second was for a fair wage. My third,
so help me, is to reincarnate furred

or feathered, skink or skunk, that I might *range*.

Big Stump Basin, 1981

Fallen sequoias
want to know: am I a logger? No.
"Liar, be frustrated."
A companion says, "These may not come out."
The light meter registers near-zero
deep in the Range of Light.
Cut to fall uphill,
they'd shattered.
Lumber executives turned red.
Dusk.

A Colloquy of Sorts

Executive D. Bastion Sr. gazed
out the rear sanctum in his limousine
hastening past a rotten shack appraised
at zilch. He mused toward local fellahin.

"You lust for an embowered avenue
as perfect as a Mona Lisa smile.
I own it: Bliss Court. There, according to
prole rumor, fashionable gentry file
evasive tax returns. Come on, admit
you covet daily our Mercedes Benzes,
prep school children, polyester knit
golf shirts, Sunday brunches, contact lenses.
What ecstasy. Nobody would suspect
a thing: you'd stow the rifle in your attic,
ditch your Stars and Bars, henceforth correct
your bully of a boss. Aristocratic
snob, you wouldn't need to be promoted,
being rich already. But you're poor
white trash, and bitter, waiting for your bloated
beer gut to give birth to tigers who're
destined for a joyless servitude;
your daughters, in the rabbit snare, will drudge."

"I'd not lay money on the Bastion brood,"
thought the chauffeur, an equally hard judge.
"When Dalton Jr. wrecked the Maserati
you bought, he tumbled out to register

.21 on the breathalyzer, body
an awkward truth or a non sequitur.
Your bribes—quick, massive, deft—would do to keep
his gilt name out of blotters (lucre sure
to cleanse a record), eminently cheap
compared to full tuition at Fenmoor.
He teed up on connections and played through.
Desiring a near-clone, mighty brahmin,
you unveiled a sham marriage. Well-to-do
she may be: not, however, a simpleton.
You'll get your grandson, she'll get Dalt's affairs
with company femmes till the midnight she
embraces him at the foot of the stairs,
a loaded Smith & Wesson by her knee."

Advice to a Profiteer

A wart-on-wart rococo ugliness
is unavoidable in times like these,
but that's okay. Engulf it in a dress
of wart-on-wart rococo ugliness,
and you'll have caught the low road to success.
Then schmooze around, spend zillions, and reprise . . .

That wart-on-wart rococo ugliness
will prove quite salable in times like these.

The Grand Exhibition

Tossed in a celebration of right size,
confetti derelicts can't see to rummage
a trashbin for pizza crust. Men stumble on
chilblain, kindergarten notions long assumed
extinct; bleed; husband energy
to retch. Flickering at drunk comrades,
a streetlamp braves kids pelting it with snowballs,
and shriveled ladies upstairs curse the noise
while fingering their broken thermostats.
An old vet snores below his crucifix.
He dreams the Eiffel Tower is melted down
for coins. His landlord is in the dream, too,
demanding payment but allowing him
to keep one penny for each mucous eye.

The Voice in No Man's Land

A yellow femur in the oozing wall
protruded, hazard, half another inch
to eavesdrop on ancestral melody.
Men violated consciously a stern
dictum and scrambled to the firestep.
Largesse of angled light at 8 p.m.
illuminated wreckage: rusty helmets,
bullet-pierced; loose strands of wire, barbed;
a cratered landscape hiding Norway rats
in competition with the morning salvage;
under rainwater, fruits of over-the-top
strategy loved by clean, mustachioed,
and absent generals (each outranked man
stumbled to his unromantic death
as if to prove the 19th century
extinct—each reduced to molecules,
cut down by a line of Maxim guns
hot enough to civilly brew tea in);
gassed, splintered, lead-filled trees where nutriment
had flourished at decade's root—soft grass
and violets underfoot, the Mérino,
a sheepdog guided by the whistling
of a shepherd as if God were possible.
No man, however he craned, saw the source.
A beautiful soprano's aria
rose, aural mist, off crucified earth. Yet
the rational thought: "It's a trick hills play,
a milkmaid in the distance wandering

home. Prevailing currents blow a sound—
artillery, for instance—straight to Kent.
The ghost cannon." (Howitzers, quite real,
spattering decision left to rot
until, piece on journalistic piece,
truth infiltrated hearts across the Channel.)
Monastic quiet. One private ran
a whispery nib's ink onto paper. Thus
a fragile mood survived the battle, a sodden
draft in the pocket of a trampled coat
days on: "She—an Angel of Mons again?—
reminded us of when the enemy
spontaneously embraced life, desperate
for Christmas even though their high command
sent Tannenbäume lit in every trench.
Lines came forward, tentatively. Then
our plum pudding and their German lager
made a festival. We toasted health
to soldiery stuck at the Western Front
and caroled in grand fashion as if possessed.
Capping gaiety our own C.O.s
bestowed the prospect of a firing squad."
Lilt faded. The voice, blessed by those
breathing in memory to keep it warm,
failed gradually. The sky, devoid of angels,
went red that night in 1917.

Sundial

Across a boulevard that might have been
annexed as rural in 1945,
before its modicum of postwar growth,
our stockyard empties. Prodded up the ramp,
beef cattle scent long-buried fear crept out
of each grave. Gnomon to a radial
arrangement of white marble (upright style),
one soldier lifts his bronze arm—patina
for olive drab—as if to question. Vein-
blue sky pumps to artery-red.
Cicadas keen in oaks. Half moon hangs pallid,
muscle on a hook, a piece of earth.

Shrapnel

Their steel-fed bodies, registered with cold,
lay in the street. Glass, randomized. A rigged-up
bomb was now a victim, too, although
it had no heaven. And the man who did
was up there now, according to his Book.
"Ironic," thought the soldier keeping peace.

Birthright

Chance. Hylo. Plenty. Best. Lura. Even.
As if from an obscure parable,
these were the names grandfather Andrew Frederick
William, who left Aargau as a boy,
chose for American offspring, against
the European urge to advertise
a peasant's loyalty to kings and queens.
I am the son of Plenty,
who never saw his hometown's black soil without sighing;
who reminisced about the house he matured in:
Best repairing its gabled roof before the Second World War,
how the parlor piano (which attracted dust
and Sunday *Post-Dispatches* in my time)
had last been played in 1933
at his grandmother's home funeral;
who furrowed garden loam each day after his office closed;
who paid my college tuition.
I delved in anthropology, resolved
to glean every move as he oiled the walker's plow,
to tape-record the family raconteur.

Too soon: father strapped onto a hospital
bed, tube-pierced, anonymous to nurses,
we of common name vigilant
to comfort him, our mother, and ourselves.
(Mother had made sure the offbeat christening
stopped. We were, therefore: David, Linda, Mark.)

Then burial and, weeks later, a yard sale:
tools Bill Blaeuer bequeathed I never learned
to swing, to dig with, to cut with, to clean.
Even so, I kept several, hoping . . .

Yet I salvaged what father salvaged:
the handle's grain one generation darker.

Parable

Inseparable, the two lamps visited
their light upon each other every day.
The one said life is good, the other said
it might improve with more égalité.
One used a curly bulb, the other had
an incandescent ideology.
Yet both were blind. If they had tried to see
the truth, they couldn't have. *Well, that's too bad:*
a pair of stupid objects. Life plugs on
with photosynthesis and clouds of spawn,
the remnants of a rogue intelligence
held in thick darkness at the bottom of
rank puddles, under rocks, in aliens
from solar systems where there is no love.

Fable

Connections popped and loosed,
the newel heads
rose like a pair of tiny oaken spaceships,
railing lifted, floated
down into a foyer, shattered a fanlight, and zoomed out
toward—miles off—one Otto Particle,
who'd gotten up and urinated, eaten
toast, then reassumed a fetal sleep.
His dogs, however, woke him with their barking,
and he opened the Venetian blinds
to witness terrorism. In his robe
he heard the brownish orbs cry, "Death to Otto!"
The banister became a battering
ram, and his front door, hollow as a straw,
mostly veneer—bought for the visual
effect it offered, not for inner strength—
burst into splinters.
He tried to reach his patio:
the back door wouldn't budge. He'd always meant to fix
that. Otto was impaled.

Forensic staff collected evidence
and measurements, hi-res shots documenting
spatter angle, wood grain. Papers asked,
who was this Particle? A cipher, really,
and the military cleared itself—
no weapon-testing anywhere, at least
not with a banister and finials.
The public was inclined to miracle:
these suckerfish now spawned a deity,
which faded to a legend and a great
advertisement for solid oak construction.

Jeremiad

The pessimists are prophets in disguise,
tut-tutting at society's decay.
The optimists are Pollyanna-wise,
intent on manufacturing surprise:
a novel climate opens every day.
The pessimists are prophets in disguise,
and I'm one, confident that if the skies
are staying up, it doesn't follow (a)
that optimists are Pollyanna-*wise*
or (b) that humans won't earn their demise
in yet another horrifying way.
The pessimists are prophets in disguise,
alright: we stand for reason. I advise
a ton of resignation also. Pray,
you optimists, you Pollyanna-wise,
to Mammon's oil. His anthracitic eyes
are gimleting your final Chevrolet.

Proof

Exhausted every
night, 70 mph
to and from a lousy job
every day,
year after year,

he prays for death.

Next day
his car battery dies.

The Road Taken

I don't remember what was down this road,
or why I took it, or when. I believe
it must have been about this time of year:
maple seeds were flying, and the cattle
avoided wallowing in the cold stream.
The woods were not quite yellow; Black Eyed Susans
were, yet. Just like now, clouds of gravel
blinded me. And wasn't there a dead end?
A road like any other—little difference.
In fact it made so small an impression on me,
I have no choice but to follow it again.

Lure

Off this or that
point.
Aluminum angles
naked, day

split by the whirring reel,
a down-home
plunk
at line's end.

Ripples
in placid water.
Sun casts monofilament—
gold leader,

its bait the world,
shadow at bay.
I
don't resist.

Methought I Saw My Late A-Soused Haint

Chilled, cowering behind a serifed R
in this recurrent dream with a deep chute
beneath, I press a button to reboot
the Morphean and surface at Hack's Bar
outside of Paradise. The avatar
of night lays hold: I'm blind and dissolute,
John Milton angering a leather-brute
with BELIAL tattooed across one scar.
I gravitate toward *the piety*
of volleyball (a chanted phrase), pale wit
spiked over the front line: 11-3.
Aware now of some military bit—
La Marseillaise—I sing, reluctantly,
until Charles Baudelaire tells me to quit.

About the Author

Mark Blaeuer's poems and occasional translations of Spanish-language poems have appeared in nearly seventy literary journals over the past four decades. His B.A. was from Illinois College, with an M.A. in anthropology from the University of Arkansas. He worked as an archeologist (both field and lab) in Illinois, Pennsylvania, and Arkansas. He spent a quarter-century interpreting nature and culture for visitors at parks and museums in Illinois, Colorado, Utah, and Arkansas. He is now a member of the Society for American Baseball Research, focusing on the diamond history of Hot Springs, Arkansas. He and his wife Sharon live on several acres with assorted rescue dogs and cats, a few miles southwest of Hot Springs.

Made in the USA
San Bernardino, CA
01 October 2014